Buzby goes sk

Severn House Paperbacks

Buzby was trying out his new skateboard. It was fun.

BUZBY

'Hi,' he called to his friends who were watching him, 'this is great!'

A little way down the street a sign had been placed in front of a hole in the pavement.
Buzby was too busy showing off to notice it.

DANGER
ROADWORKS

Crash! Buzby hit the roadworks sign. The skateboard flew into the air and landed on one of the flashing lights. Buzby fell head over heels into the hole.

DANGER
ROADWORKS

Seeing the accident, Buzby's friends dashed to a phone box and one of them dialled 999.
'Fire, Police or Ambulance?' asked the operator.
'Ambulance! Emergency! Buzby's fallen down a hole!'
'Where are you speaking from?' asked the operator.
'The phone box on the corner of Station Road and High Street,' replied Buzby's friend.
'Station Road and High Street,' repeated the operator.
'The Ambulance will come immediately.'

S-Z
A-D

In a few minutes, the ambulance arrived.
'Were you skateboarding?' asked the ambulance man. 'You should know better than to do that in the street.'
He lifted Buzby onto a stretcher and soon they were speeding off to hospital.

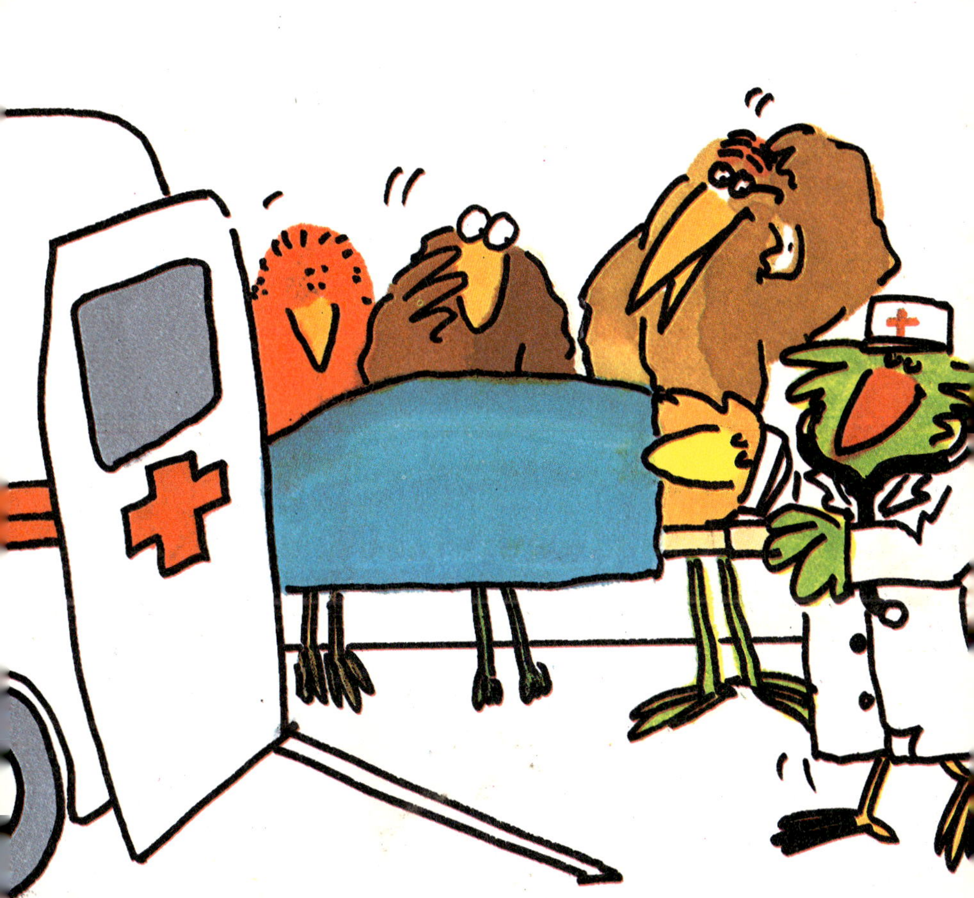

The doctor decided Buzby was not seriously hurt. He had only sprained his ankle, but he was badly bruised and very shaken up.

'Better keep you in hospital for a few days just to be sure,' he said.

The nurse wasn't very sympathetic. She thought he should have been wearing his protective gear.

When Buzby felt better, he phoned his Mother.
'Hello Mum,' he said, 'I'm in hospital.' He explained what had happened.
'Oh Buzby! You are a naughty boy. You know you shouldn't go skateboarding in the street.'
'Sorry Mum.'
'Now Buzby,' she said 'just you get a helmet and some knee and elbow pads before you go skate-boarding again.'
'Yes Mum,' said Buzby.

The next day his friends came to visit him.
'Hello, Buzby. We've brought you a present,' they said as they crowded round the bed. Buzby unwrapped the parcel.
'A helmet and pads! Oooh, thanks,' he said, trying them on.
'Now Buzby,' said the nurse, 'no excuse for skate-boarding without a helmet and pads!'
'Thanks a lot,' repeated Buzby. He was really pleased.
'See you at the skateboard park, Buzby, when you're better!' they said.

Buzby was soon up and about again. He joined his friends at the park.

SKATEBOARD PARK
BUZBY

As they were leaving the park, Buzby saw a notice on the wall. A Skateboard Championship was to be held and there were to be several different events.

NOTICE BOARD
SKATEBOARD CHAMPIONSHIPS SATURDAY

They all discussed the championships over milk-shakes in the local cafe. Each of Buzby's friends planned to enter one event, but Buzby wanted to go in for all of them. He suggested they should also enter the team race.

ecream

They practised every day until Saturday. The free-style event was very difficult but Buzby managed to come second.

BUZBY

In the slalom race all the competitors began well. Buzby however lost balance and fell off his skate-board. The other competitors tried to avoid him but unsuccessfully. They all bumped into each other and landed in a heap. Everyone was disqualified.

BUZBY

They had been practising for the team event all week. They tried hard and their performance was perfect. When the teams had finished, the judge announced the winner.
'The winner of the team event is . . . The Buzby Team!'
Buzby held the cup high for the crowd to see.
'Well done, Buzby,' they cheered.

BUZBY

BUZBY GOES SKATEBOARDING

SEVERN HOUSE PAPERBACKS LIMITED, 1979
144–146 New Bond Street, London W1Y 9FD

ISBN 0 906461 00 6
ISBN 0 906461 09 X (Display Pack only)

Made and printed in Great Britain by William Clowes & Sons, Limited London, Beccles and Colchester